A Place on the Team

Sheila M. Blackburn

The sixth book in Set A of
Sam's Football Stories

Dedication
For My Mum.
With thanks to Tom for all the support
and understanding.

Ackowledgements
With thanks to *The Boots Company* and *Delmar Press in Nantwich*,
for their support of this project.

Published by Brilliant Publications
1 Church View
Sparrow Hall Farm
Edlesborough
Dunstable
Beds LU6 2ES

Telephone: 01525 229720
Fax: 01525 229725
e-mail: sales@brilliantpublications.co.uk
website: www.brilliantpublications.co.uk

Written by Sheila M. Blackburn
Illustrated by Tony O'Donnell of Graham Cameron Illustration

© Sheila M. Blackburn 2002

ISBN 1 903853 192 Set A – 6 titles: Football Crazy, Team Talk, Will Monday Ever Come?, Training Night, If Only Dad Could See Us! and A Place on the Team.
ISBN 1 903853 036 Set B – 6 titles: The First Match, Trouble for Foz, What about the Girls?, What's Worrying Eddie?, Nowhere to Train and Are We the Champions?

Printed in England by Ashford Colour Press Ltd
First published in 2002
10 9 8 7 6 5 4 3 2 1

The right of Sheila Blackburn to be identified as the author of this work have been
asserted by her in accordance with the Copyright, Designs and Patents Act 1988.

Eddie got all the boys together in the big room
after training that Monday. This was the moment
they had all been waiting for –
news of who would be in the team for the first match.

"Our first match will be on Sunday," Eddie began.

There were some mums and dads in the room, waiting for their boys. Everyone wanted to hear Eddie's plans.

"Now that we've done a few training sessions, I have fixed up a friendly match. We will play Parton Rovers on Sunday at 10.30am. It's to be an away match, because they have a good pitch."

Some of the lads cheered.
Sam felt really excited and pleased.
Even if he didn't make it into the team,
it had all been his idea in the first place.

PARTON ROV
SUNDAY
at
10.30am

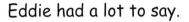

Eddie had a lot to say.

"I've picked a team," he went on.
"We'll play 11 a-side with two subs.
I'm sorry that you can't all play.
Perhaps some of you will come to support us."

The lads were looking at each other.
They all wanted to be in the team.

"If you are playing, please make your own way
there. Parton is on the other side of town. I can
tell you the way if you need help." Eddie went on,
"There are two more things before I read the team
list out. About your kit ... "

"I was thinking about that too," Sam said to Danny.
"I wonder what it'll be."

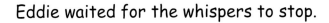

Eddie waited for the whispers to stop.

"If lads in the team can bring black shorts,
Mr Bond says we can borrow the school's shirts
and bibs. Leave all of that to me."

Danny looked at Sam.
"The first team has two strips," he said.
"I hope we get the red and black one."

"How do you know we'll be in the team?" Sam said.

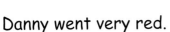

Danny went very red.
"I mean – I hope our new team gets the red one!"

Sam smiled. He knew what Danny meant.
He wanted to be in the team just as much,
but they both knew that some lads had to be dropped.
It was hard waiting to find out.

"The last thing to think about is a team name,"
said Eddie.

"Who will choose?" one of the dads asked. "Will it just be the lads in the team this week?"

Eddie nodded. "Good point," he said.
"I think we should all have a say. If you're not in the team this week, you'll play for the team another time. So, we should all get a chance to choose."

It sounded fair.

Eddie asked them to wait a bit longer.

He said they could have a vote.

"I'm sure some of you have already been thinking about a name," he said. "So I'll put all your ideas down and then we'll have the vote."

This was really good.
Eddie did have some really good plans.

Lee put his hand up first.
"What about Newton Rovers?" he said.

Eddie wrote it down.

"Or Newton Rangers," said Ali.

That went down too.

Sam said the name could be Newton Albion.

"Thanks," said Eddie.
"I need about three more on the list."

"Newton Under Tens?" said one of the dads.

Eddie was busy writing.

Newton United was another idea.

"I should have guessed!" said Eddie with a grin.

Somebody else said: "Newton Devils."

"Thank you all," said Eddie.
"We have six names now. Time to vote."

Eddie gave each of the boys a pencil
and a slip of paper. He read out the names again and
gave each name a number.

"Now you don't have to worry about your spelling,"
he said.

"Thank goodness for that!" said Danny.

Eddie began to explain the rules:
"If you like Newton Rovers as a name, put the number 1 on your slip.

Newton Rangers is number 2.

Newton Albion is 3.

Newton Under Tens is 4.

Newton United is 5.

and Newton Devils is number 6."

It was quiet in the big room for a few minutes.

"Right," said Eddie.
"I'll collect the slips.
There are sixteen boys here tonight,
so I need to collect sixteen slips."

Eddie went round the room, taking the slips of paper. He put them on a table and began reading them.

He was making little piles of slips, one for each team number.

It wasn't long before he was ready.

The boys were sitting quietly for once.

Sam's Football Stories

"OK – here are the results:

Name 1	Newton Rovers	1 vote
Name 2	Newton Rangers	2 votes
Name 3	Newton Albion	2 votes
Name 4	Newton Under Tens	0 votes
Name 5	Newton United	3 votes
Name 6	Newton Devils	8 votes."

Danny gasped.
"Fancy that! It's not United."

"There's only one United!" Sam said.
"We don't want to get mixed up!"

"Thank you, lads," Eddie was saying.
"I like this name a lot. The Scouts need to come in now, so I'll read out the team and then we must go home."

There was a real hush round the room.

Eddie read:

Goal:	Rob
Defence:	Lee, Tim, Chip, Ali
Mid-field:	Ben, Mouse, Jon
Forwards:	Sam, Foz, Danny
Subs:	Mo, Leroy."

Sam closed his eyes.
He had got his first place in a real football team!

"Goodnight, then, Newton Devils!
See you on Sunday – don't be late!"

Eddie left the room.

Some of the boys went out with their mums
and dads.

Sam sat very still.
He didn't want to spoil this moment.
It was very special.
He knew he would always remember it.

"I really think the red shirts
would be good," Danny said again.
"With a name like Devils, we need to play in red."

Sam's dad came over.

"Don't you like the name, Danny?" Dad asked.

"Yes – I do," said Danny.
"Well, I really like United as a name.
Sam's right. We could get mixed up with the
real United."

"We'll have to wait till Sunday to see about that,"
said Dad. "Now, come on, you two. Let's go."

It was getting dark outside.

Some of the Scouts were leaning
against the wall, talking.

Eddie was standing outside in his tracksuit.

He saw Sam with his dad and Danny.

"Well done, lads," he said. "Are you pleased?"

"You bet!" said Danny.

Eddie climbed on his old bike and pedalled off.

Sam was very quiet on the way home.
He was thinking.

Danny did all the talking.
"It's a good team, I reckon," he said.
"He's picked the right forward line-up.
We did do well tonight – and that last minute cross
was really wicked, Sam. If we play like that on
Sunday, we'll kill them!"

Dad smiled as they walked.
He had been just like this when he was a boy.
Picking the right team is always so important.

"Rob's a good goalie," Danny went on.
"Tim was pretty solid in defence.
He'll be fine with Chip.
Don't know much about Lee and Ali.
They're in Mrs Day's class ...
Talking of chips – I'm hungry. I could just do with
some chips."

"We've got to get you home!
Never mind chips," said Dad, laughing.

Danny talked on and on.

Sam just nodded.

At last, they got to Danny's house.

"Bye then, Danny," said Dad.
"I'm going to see your grandad at the hospital
tomorrow. I'll make sure I tell him everything."

"Thanks," said Danny. "I know Grandad will be
really pleased. Bye."

Danny turned to face Sam. "I'm really glad I went
tonight, Sam. Thanks for getting me to go. See you
tomorrow."

He ran into the house, calling his mum to tell her
the news – and to ask her what he could have to eat.

A Place on the Team

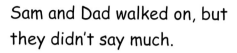

Sam and Dad walked on, but
they didn't say much.

Mum was surprised that Sam was so quiet.

"You must have a lot to tell me, Sam," she said.
"You always do after training."

"Well, yes, I do," said Sam.

He sat down at the kitchen table
for a drink of hot chocolate.

"Don't you feel excited?" Dad asked.
"You're very quiet."

"I'm just so pleased," said Sam.
"I've wanted to be in a real football team for
such a long time. Now I can hardly believe it!"

"You'd better believe it, Sam," said Dad.
"I saw the end of the game tonight.
You played very well. You should have seen his
cross to Foz,"
he said to Mum.

"Sam, tell Mum about the team," Dad went on.
"Danny was right. Eddie has picked a good team –
and a great forward line-up."

He stopped, waiting for Sam to say something.

Sam sat looking at his mug of hot chocolate.
"It's just as if I'm dreaming," was all he could say.

"No – I can promise you, you're not dreaming, but you soon will be," said Dad.

"Finish your drink, Sam – it's time for a bath."

"I made it!" Sam said with a big grin.

"Yes, you did, Sam. Well done!"

We hope that you enjoyed this book. To find out what happens next, look for the next book in the series.

Set A
Football Crazy
Team Talk
Will Monday Ever Come?
Training Night
If Only Dad Could See Us!
A Place on the Team

Set B
The First Match
Trouble for Foz
What about the Girls?
What's Worrying Eddie?
Nowhere to Train
Are We the Champions?